*War Memorials*

# WORLD WAR I
# MEMORIAL

## Maureen Picard Robins

ROURKE PUBLISHING

Vero Beach, Florida 32964

www.rourkepublishing.com

Photo credits: © Randomphotog: Title Page; © Dean Bergman: 4, 25; © Library of Congress: 5, 6, 7, 8, 9, 10, 11, 12, 13, 14, ; © US Department of Defense: 11; © Chris Pritchard: 15, 18, 19, 23; © Wikipedia: 16. 20, 26; © Michael Westhoff: 17; © Jennifer Trenchard: 21; © Associated Press: 27

Editor: Kelli Hicks

Cover and Interior design by Tara Raymo

Library of Congress Cataloging-in-Publication Data

Robins, Maureen Picard.
  World War I memorial / Maureen Picard Robins.
      p. cm. -- (War memorials)
  Includes bibliographical references and index.
  ISBN 978-1-60694-427-1
  1. Liberty Memorial (Kansas City, Mo.)--Juvenile literature. 2. Kansas City
(Mo.)--Buildings, structures, etc.--Juvenile literature. 3. Magonigle, Harold
Van Buren, 1867-1935--Juvenile literature. I. Title. II. Title: World War One
memorial. III. Title: World War 1 memorial.
  D675.K2R63 2010
  940.4'65778411--dc22
                                    2009005886

Printed in the USA

CG/CG

**ROURKE PUBLISHING**

www.rourkepublishing.com - rourke@rourkepublishing.com
Post Office Box 643328  Vero Beach, Florida 32964

# Table of Contents

"IN HONOR OF THOSE WHO SERVED IN THE WORLD WAR IN DEFENSE OF LIBERTY AND OUR COUNTRY."

*Inscription on the Liberty Memorial tower in downtown Kansas City, Missouri, U.S.*

# The Great War

The Great War (1914-1918) was the world's first **global** conflict. American soldiers left home to fight in faraway places in Europe and many never returned.

The War began with the assassination of Archduke Franz Ferdinand, **heir** to the throne of Austria-Hungary. He was **assassinated** in Sarajevo on June 28, 1914.

In reaction, Austria-Hungary immediately declared war on Serbia. Within the next months, Germany would declare war on Russia, France, and Belgium. By January, 1915, it seemed as though the entire world was at war.

Soldiers protected themselves from gunfire by digging holes called trenches, and hiding in them. The military also used tanks and other new weapons to try and gain an advantage over the enemy.

5

Historians believe that there were several causes of this Great War. Germany, a young power, had new leadership and decided not to renew its friendship with Russia. The European countries were also experiencing growth of industry and technology. They were interested in expanding their wealth and territories. This upset the balance of power and created both new alliances and great conflict.

Ireland

Great
Britain

Norway

Denmark

Sweden

*North Sea*

*Baltic*

Netherlands

Germany

Belgium

Luxembourg

*Bay
of
Biscay*

France

Switzerland

Liech.

Austro-Hungarian
Empire

Romania

*Black Sea*

Italy

Serbia

Mont.

Bulgaria

Albania

Greece

Ottoman
Empire

*Mediterranean Sea*

..in

*American soldiers, nicknamed doughboys, fought the enemy along the
borders of Germany, France, and Belgium in 1917.*

7

The warring European nations organized into two groups.
The Allies included Belgium, France, Great Britain, Russia,
and Serbia. The United States would join them in 1917.
Austria-Hungary, Germany, and the Ottoman Empire made
up the Central Power countries.

Many of these battles were focused on 466 miles
(750 kilometers) in Europe called The Western Front.

Norway

Denmark

Sweden

*North Sea*

*Baltic*

Ireland

Great
Britain

Netherlands

Germany

Belgium

Luxembourg

**The Western Front**

*Bay
of
Biscay*

France

Switzerland   Liech.

Austro-Hungarian
Empire

Romania

*Black Sea*

Italy

Serbia

Mont.

Bulgaria

Albania

Greece

Ottoman
Empire

*Mediterranean Sea*

*In 1918, the Allies were finally able to stop the German advance at
the Western Front and begin to push the enemy back.*

On November 11, 1918, a cease fire was declared. That day, originally called **Armistice Day,** now known as Veteran's Day, called for rejoicing and world wide celebrations of peace.

When the celebrations stopped, people considered ways to mourn their lost patriots and to remember their sacrifices. People wanted to express lessons learned from such **devastation.**

In Europe, battlefields were turned into cemeteries with memorials.

*Flanders Field was the site of some of the Great War's bloodiest battles.*

The Flanders Field American Cemetery is located in Belgium on the battlefield where the U.S. 91st Division suffered many casualties.

II

# A Great Response

Within days of the Armistice, the citizens of Kansas City, Missouri, decided to build a memorial to its war heroes. They imagined a great and beautiful memorial. It was going to be a lasting reminder, in the heartland of America, of so many who traveled to fight the enemy in the fields of Belgium and France.

DEDICATED · NOVEMBER · 1 · 1921
IN THE PRESENCE OF
MARSHAL FOCH · ADMIRAL BEATTY · GENERAL PERSHING
GENERAL DIAZ · GENERAL JACQUES
VICE PRESIDENT CALVIN COOLIDGE
ROBERT ALEXANDER LONG
PRESIDENT OF THE LIBERTY MEMORIAL ASSOCIATION

GUESTS OF THE AMERICAN LEGION

Civic leader and businessman, Robert Alexander Long, formed the Liberty Memorial Association, a group of men and women who would decide what kind of memorial to build. The committee set a $2 million goal (estimated to be about $40 million in today's currency) and within two weeks the money was raised.

# Who Will Design the Memorial?

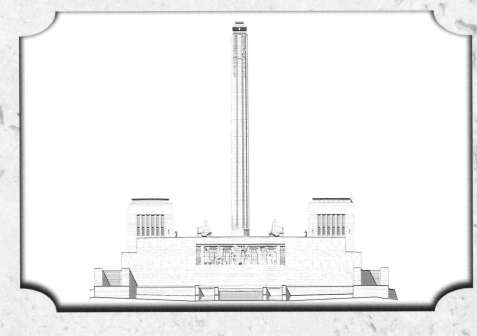

Long wanted to satisfy many people so he, along with other city leaders, decided to hold a competition. The competition began in February, 1921, and eleven architects submitted entries. The winner was Harold Van Buren Magonigle, an architect from New York City.

His design was grand. An **eternal** flame called the Flame of Inspiration would burn on top of a tower. His design spoke of the Dawn of Peace.

*Union Station, Kansas City*

He wanted to build the memorial on a hill just south of Kansas City's new Union Station. He liked this spot because the memorial would be very tall and therefore visible from great distances. The height of the building would also create deep shadows on the ground.

Not everyone was pleased that an out of town architect won the design competition. But, everyone agreed that his design was the best.

# The Great Plan

A tall limestone tower lies at the center of the memorial. It is surrounded by two small buildings and is guarded by two enormous stone sphinxes.

These elements are arranged **symmetrically** so that one half of the memorial mirrors the other.

*H. Van Buren Magonigle said he borrowed images from the bible so that his tower would offer a "pillar of clouds by day and a pillar of fire by night to lead men out of bondage and strife into the promised land of peace."*

# A Tour of the Memorial

*Guardian Spirit of Sacrifice*

Near the top of the tower are four sculptures, each one being 40 feet (12.19 meters) tall and carved into the limestone. These giant Guardian Spirits possess individual personalities and symbolize important parts of the American character. Honor wears a **laurel** wreath. Courage wears a helmet and Patriotism wears a civic crown. Finally, there is Sacrifice who has a winged star on her forehead.

### *Flame of Inspiration*

Magonigle wanted the tower to have a cloud overhead by day and a flame at night. He designed a Flame of Inspiration. His idea was to send steam, made from boilers in the basement, to the roof. This steam, by day, would create a cloud effect. At night, three rings of white, orange, and red light bulbs would shine and their light would reflect off the steam creating the impression of real fire.

### The Sphinxes

Twin stone **sphinxes,** named Memory and Future, guard the southern entrance of the memorial site. A typical Egyptian sphinx has the head of a man and the body, legs, feet, and tail of a lion. Greek sphinxes are traditionally sculpted with the head of a woman.

The memorial's sphinxes are considered Greek in style. Memory's winged arm covers her face protecting her from seeing the horrors of war. She faces east, pointing in the direction of World War I battlefields such as Flanders Field.

Future faces west, away from a vision of war. Future looks to the years ahead which cannot be seen.

## The Halls

The two smaller buildings, called Memory Hall and Exhibition Hall, complete this symmetrical site plan.

Memory Hall, on the east side, contains bronze tablets etched with the names of Kansas City residents who died in World War I. There are also many murals in Memory Hall.

The building to the west, Exhibition Hall, shows portions of a mural, Pantheon de la Guerre, as well as a British Naval gun, and an Allied flag collection.

21

The North Frieze was very important to Magonigle and he selected his wife, Edith, to paint the story of war. He planned to translate Edith's paintings into a sculpted wall. This plan worried the Liberty Committee. First, they weren't convinced that Edith was the right person to do this work. Second, it was very expensive. Edith completed her drawings called *The March of Civilization* but it took nine years! These drawings were never realized in stone.

The committee eventually hired Edmond Amateis to carve **relief** images that reveal the process from war to peace. It stretches 400 feet (121 meters) and stands 13 feet (3.9 meters) high.

The North Frieze was an object of compromise as R.A. Long, who controlled the budget, asked the architect, H. Van Buren Magonigle to reconsider the plans and its expense.

# Restoration and a New Museum

In 1994, the memorial was closed to the public because its concrete and structures had badly deteriorated. In 1998, Kansas City residents passed a sales tax to raise 30 million dollars for restoration of the memorial and another 14.7 million to create an **endowment** for upkeep and maintenance.

The restoration of the memorial was necessary to keep the memorial **vital.** It was also an opportunity to add a museum. New architects carved space beneath the memorial tower to create The National World War I Museum. The museum opened in 2006.

The four spirits atop the tower were sculpted by Richard Aiken. The spirits are symbolic reminders of The Great War's purpose and the heroism of the generation.

Since its completion in 1921, the memorial has been a Kansas City and national monument, looking over the downtown skyline. The museum has been designated by Congress as the nation's official World War I Museum, and it is the first and only American museum solely dedicated to preserving the objects, history, and personal experiences of a war whose impact still echoes in our world today.

*The entrance to the National World War I museum opens to a field of mock poppies as a reminder of the sacrifices made at Flanders Field and the imagery from the famous poem,* In Flanders Fields.

27

# Timeline

**June 28, 1914** — Archduke Franz Ferdinand and his wife are assassinated in Sarajevo.

**April, 1917** — United States declares war on Germany and joins the war on the side of the Allies.

**November 11, 1918** — Armistice is signed and World War I ends.

**December, 1918** — Community led fundraising drive raises over $2,500,000.

**1920** — Women get the right to vote with the passing of the 19th Amendment.

**1920-1922** — War cemeteries created on war fronts. War memorials are dedicated in villages and cities at home.

**November 1, 1924** —— Liberty memorial opens after three years of construction.

**November 11, 1935** —— The North Frieze is completed.

**1998** —— Kansas City residents vote to pass a half-cent sales tax to fund a restoration of the historic landmark.

**2004** —— Kansas city residents approve a bond issue to construct a world-class museum at the memorial.

**May 2002** —— The Liberty Memorial reopens.

**December 2006** —— The World War I museum opens.

29

# Fun Facts

★ A limestone tower is the heart of the memorial. It soars 217 feet 6 inches (66.29 meters) into the sky.

★ The sphinxes weigh 600 tons.

★ The site is also oriented 11 degrees off true north, as a tribute to the signing of the Armistice or cease fire at 11:00 a.m. on November 11, 1918.

★ Wings appear throughout the memorial in various ways. There are wings on the Guardian Spirits and the Sphinxes. Eagles are also a decorative element found at the site. The wing motif was also added to the larger design of the building. For every eight feet of height, the walls angle back one inch.

★ The annual cost to keep the flame burning is currently estimated to be $45,000 by officials at the National World War I Museum at Liberty Memorial.

# Glossary

**assassinate** (uh-SASS-uh-nate) : to murder someone who is well-known or important

**armistice** (ARM-iss-tiss): a temporary agreement to stop fighting a war

**Armistice Day** (ARM-iss-tiss day): November 11, 1918, the day the fighting stopped in Europe

**devastation** (DEV-uh-stay-shun): ruins or desolation due to violent action

**endowment** (en-DOW-ment): a permanent fund to provide support for a cause

**eternal** (ee-TUR-nuhl): lasting forever

**global** (GLOHB-ul): worldwide

**heir** (air): someone who has been, or will be, left money, property, or a title

**laurel** (LOR-uhl): an evergreen shrub with shiny, pointed leaves used by the ancient Greeks to crown victors in various contests

**relief** (ri-LEEF): figures or details that are raised from a surface

**symmetrically** (si-MET-ruh-kuhl-ee): having matching points, parts or shapes on both sides of a dividing line

**sphinxes** (sfingks ): monsters in mythology having a lion's body, wings, and the head of a woman

**vital** (VYE-tuhl): important or essential

31

# Index

# Websites

www.pbs.org/greatwar

www.theworldwar.org

www.firstworldwar.com/warontheweb/museums.htm

www.madison.k12.wi.us/tnl/detectives/kids/KIDS-000411.html

cyberslueth-kids/sleuth/History/Wars?World_War_I/index.htm

# About the Author

Maureen Picard Robins writes poetry and books for kids and adults. She is an assistant principal at a New York City middle school. She lives in one of the five boroughs of New York City with her husband and daughters.